MICKEY'S PRACTICE WORKBOOKS

SPELLING

Publishers · GROSSET & DUNLAP · New York

A B C D E F G
H I J K L M
N O P Q R S T
U V W X Y Z

a b c d e f g
h i j k l m
n o p q r s t
u v w x y z

Vacations

Write the words.

suitcase _Suit case_

pack _pack_

hotel _hotel_

airplane _airplane_

car _car_

bus _bus_

train _train_

beach _beach_

country _country_

city _city_

Spell the words.

bus

HOTEL

airplane

cars

qunchry

car

Spell the new words that rhyme with:

peach   **rain**   **tack**

<u>b</u>each

<u>t</u>rain

<u>p</u>ack

Write a sentence for each word.

★

suitcase I cered a suit case.

carry

carried

country I went to a country.

hotel I stayed in a hotel.

stayed

beach I went to the beach.

city I rade a car in the city.

Body

Write the words.

head _____

arms _____

legs _____

neck _____

feet _____

hand _____

fingers _____

ears _____

eyes _____

mouth _____

Spell the words.

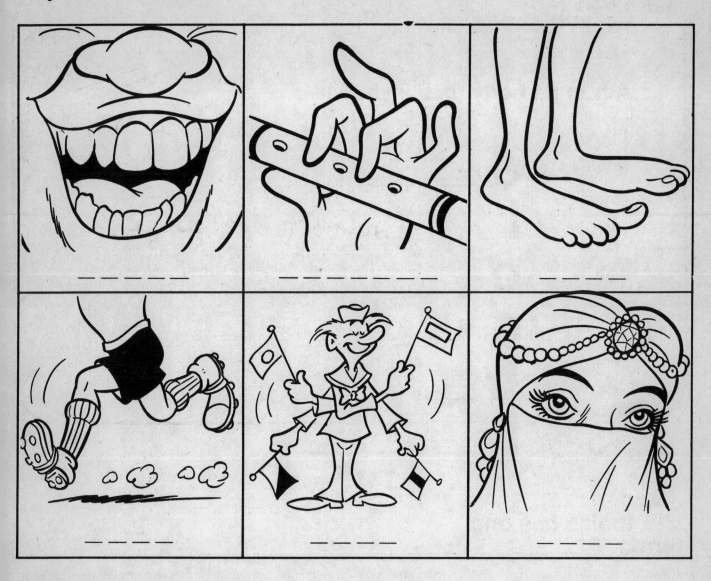

_ _ _ _ _   _ _ _ _ _ _ _   _ _ _ _ _

_ _ _ _ _   _ _ _ _ _   _ _ _ _ _

Spell the new words that rhyme with:

deck   **tears**   **sand**

_ _ _ _ _   _ _ _ _ _   _ _ _ _ _

Fill in the spaces.

A human body usually has two

a __ __ __

l __ __ __

e __ __ __

e __ r __

h __ __ __ __

f __ __ __

It also has one

h __ __ __

n __ __ __

m __ __ __ __

What does it have 10 of?

__ __ __ __ __ __ __ __ __ __

Spell the words. Check yourself.

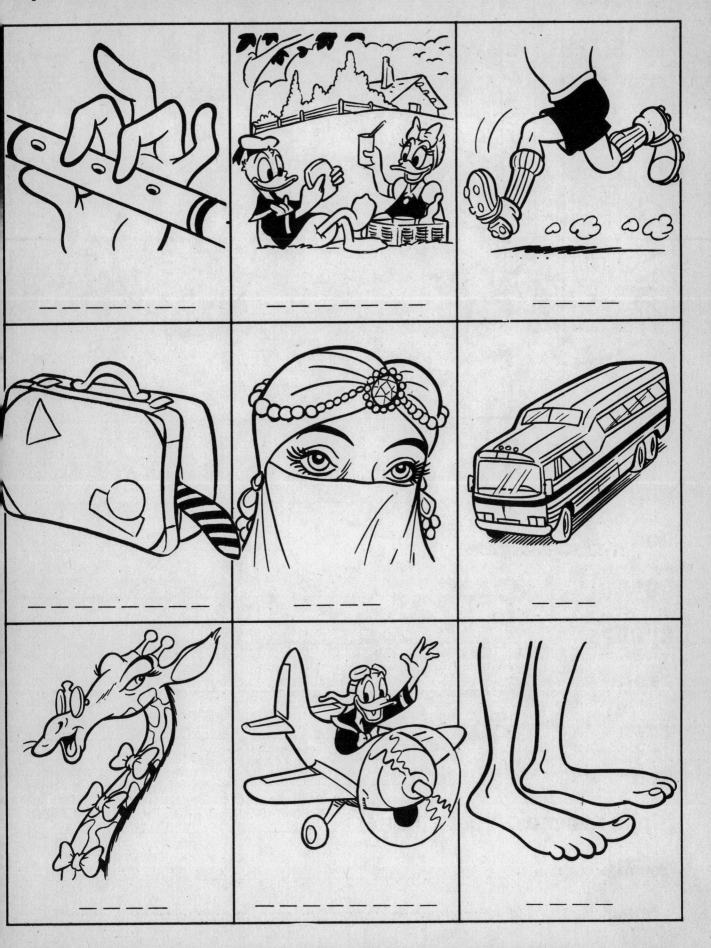

_ _ _ _ _ _ _ _

_ _ _ _ _ _ _

_ _ _ _

_ _ _ _ _ _ _ _

_ _ _

_ _ _ _

_ _ _ _ _ _ _

_ _ _ _ _ _ _ _

_ _ _ _

Zoo

Write the words.

monkey _____

lion _____

tiger _____

giraffe _____

zebra _____

deer _____

bear _____

hippopotamus _____

gorilla _____

snake _____

Spell the words.

_ _ _ _ _ _ _   _ _ _ _   _ _ _ _ _

_ _ _ _ _ _   _ _ _ _ _   _ _ _ _ _ _ _ _ _ _ _

Spell the new words that rhyme with:

pear   **donkey**   **flake**

_ _ _ _   _ _ _ _ _ _   _ _ _ _ _

Give each zoo animal a name and write about it.

tiger _____

_____

_____

_____

hippopotamus _____

_____

_____

_____

snake _____

_____

_____

_____

gorilla _____

_____

_____

_____

giraffe _____

_____

_____

Spell the words. Check yourself.

Numbers

Write the words.

one _____

two _____

three _____

four _____

five _____

six _____

seven _____

eight _____

nine _____

ten _____

Spell the words.

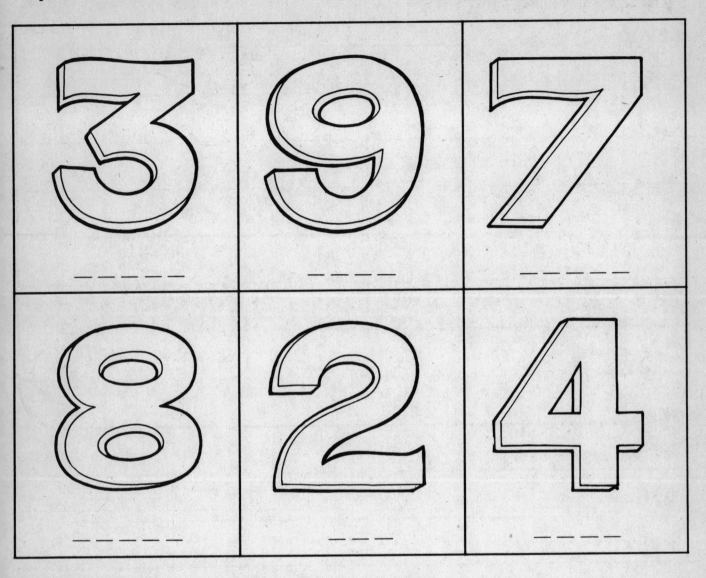

3 _ _ _ _ _

9 _ _ _ _

7 _ _ _ _ _

8 _ _ _ _ _

2 _ _ _

4 _ _ _ _

Spell the new words that rhyme with:

dive   mix   hen

_ _ _ _   _ _ _   _ _ _

Write a sentence for each word.

seven _____

_____

_____

ten _____

_____

_____

one _____

_____

_____

four _____

_____

_____

nine _____

_____

_____

Garden

Write the words.

flower _____

grass _____

soil _____

hoe _____

beetle _____

plant _____

spider _____

seed _____

bee _____

watering can _____

Spell the words.

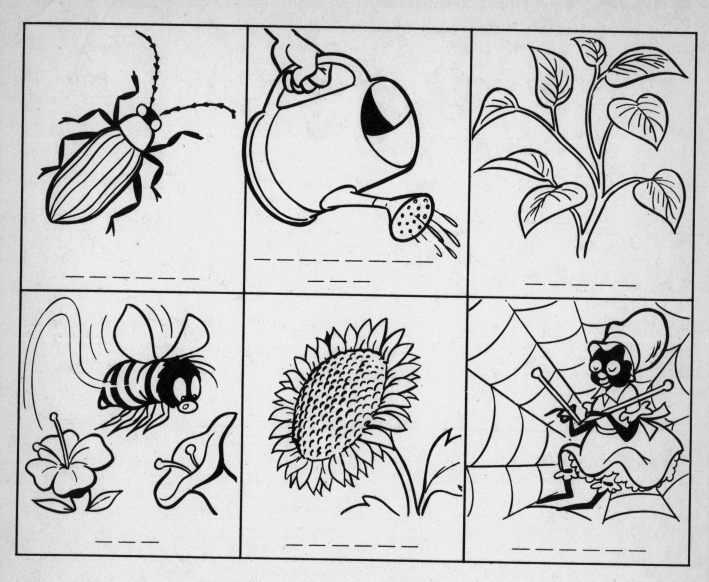

_ _ _ _ _   _ _ _ _ _   _ _ _ _ _

_ _ _ _ _   _ _ _ _ _   _ _ _ _ _ _

Spell the new words that rhyme with:

toe   glass   feed

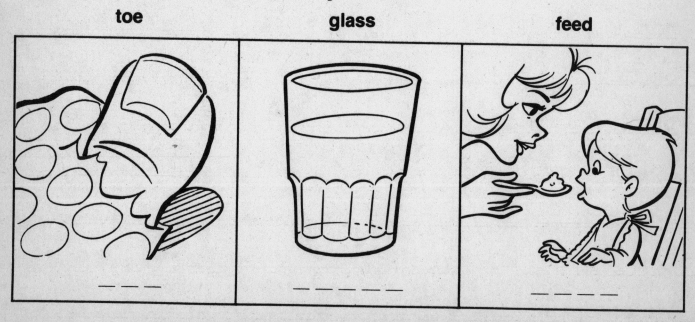

_ _ _ _ _   _ _ _ _ _   _ _ _ _ _

Write a story about the lonely garden spider.
Use these words in your sentences:

soil   **grass**   **flower**   **seed**   **bee**

_____

_____

_____

_____

_____

_____

_____

_____

_____

_____

_____

_____

Cooking

Write the words.

stove _____

oven _____

teapot _____

pan _____

roast _____

bake _____

apron _____

boil _____

food _____

dishes _____

Spell the words.

Spell the new words that rhyme with:

toast	cake	can

Spell the words. Check yourself.

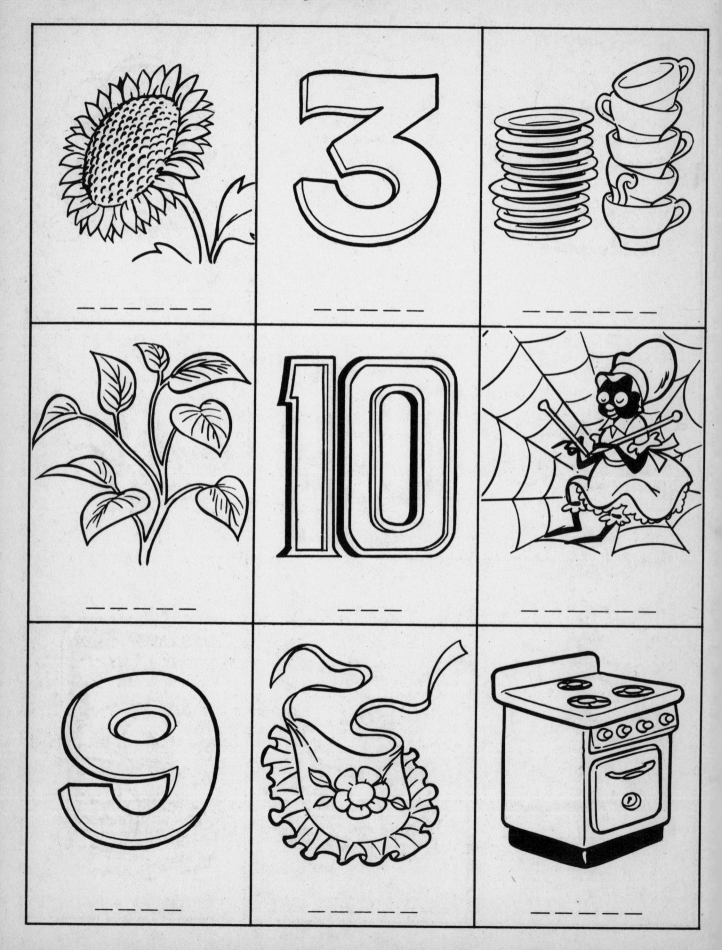

_ _ _ _ _ _ _ _ _

_ _ _ _ _

_ _ _ _ _ _ _

_ _ _ _ _ _

_ _ _ _ _

_ _ _ _ _ _ _

_ _ _ _

_ _ _ _ _ _ _

_ _ _ _ _

Spell the words. Check yourself.

Write directions for using each of these things for cooking.

stove _____

_____

_____

_____

oven _____

_____

_____

_____

apron _____

_____

_____

_____

teapot _____

_____

_____

_____

pan _____

_____

_____

_____

Clothes

Write the words.

gloves _____

coat _____

scarf _____

shoes _____

jacket _____

pants _____

skirt _____

boots _____

underwear _____

vest _____

Spell the words.

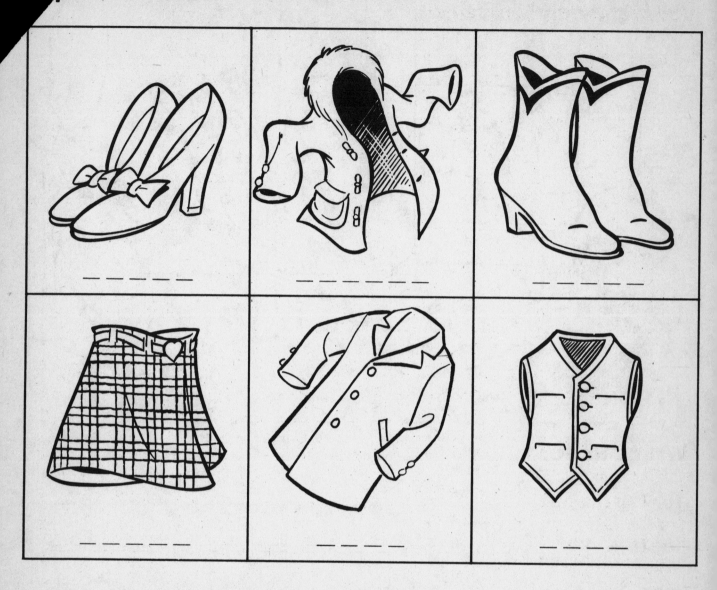

＿ ＿ ＿ ＿ ＿

＿ ＿ ＿ ＿ ＿

＿ ＿ ＿ ＿ ＿

＿ ＿ ＿ ＿ ＿

＿ ＿ ＿ ＿ ＿

＿ ＿ ＿ ＿ ＿

Spell the new words that rhyme with:

doves   plants   shirt

＿ ＿ ＿ ＿ ＿

＿ ＿ ＿ ＿ ＿

＿ ＿ ＿ ＿ ＿

Name 3 other pieces of clothing that you wear with each word.

scarf _____

_____   _____

pants _____

_____   _____

skirt _____

_____   _____

vest _____

_____   _____

jacket _____

_____   _____

Groceries

Write the words.

milk _____

eggs _____

butter _____

cheese _____

juice _____

lettuce _____

carrot _____

cereal _____

bread _____

meat _____

Spell the words.

_ _ _ _ _   _ _ _ _ _ _ _   _ _ _ _ _ _

_ _ _ _ _   _ _ _ _ _ _   _ _ _ _ _ _

Spell the new words that rhyme with:

thread   **seat**   **parrot**

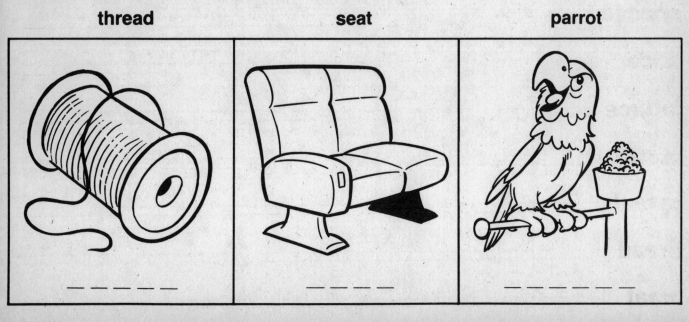

_ _ _ _ _ _   _ _ _ _   _ _ _ _ _ _

Write a story about your trip to the grocery store.
Use these words in your sentences.

cereal   bread   eggs   milk   meat

_____

_____

_____

_____

_____

_____

_____

_____

_____

_____

_____

_____

People

Write the words.

doctor _____

teacher _____

judge _____

fire fighter _____

engineer _____

baker _____

nurse _____

writer _____

mechanic _____

tailor _____

Spell the words.

Spell the new words that rhyme with:

sailor   **preacher**   **prizefighter**

Write a story about the pictures on the last page.
Use these words in your sentences:

engineer   mechanic   teacher   doctor   fire fighter

_____

_____

_____

_____

_____

_____

_____

_____

_____

_____

_____

_____

_____

_____

School

Write the words.

desk _____

pencil _____

notebook _____

blackboard _____

teacher _____

map _____

chalk _____

clock _____

flag _____

paper _____

Spell the words.

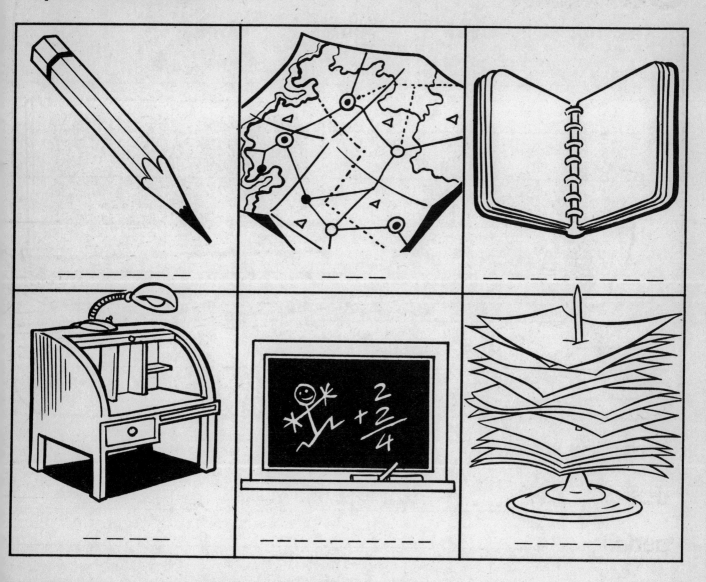

_ _ _ _ _ _

_ _ _

_ _ _ _

_ _ _ _

_ _ _ _ _ _ _ _ _

_ _ _ _ _

Spell the new words that rhyme with:

walk   bag   sock

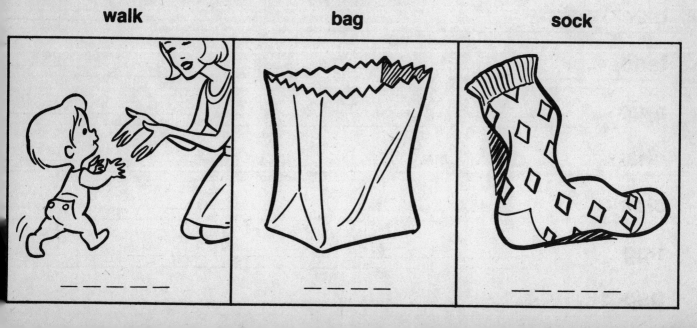

_ _ _ _

_ _ _

_ _ _

Write a story using these words in sentences:

teacher   desk   chalk   map   clock

Circus

Write the words.

tent _____

tightrope _____

ringmaster _____

clown _____

ticket _____

popcorn _____

balloon _____

elephant _____

peanuts _____

juggler _____

Spell the words.

_ _ _ _ _	_ _ _ _ _ _ _ _	_ _ _ _ _ _
_ _ _ _ _ _	_ _ _ _ _ _ _	_ _ _ _ _ _ _

Spell the new words that rhyme with:

bent   town   cricket

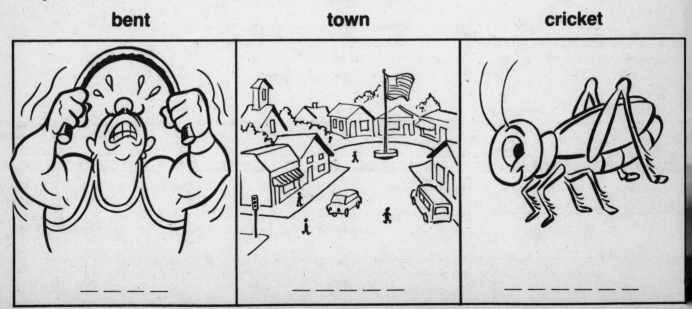

_ _ _ _	_ _ _ _ _	_ _ _ _ _ _

**Use these circus words in sentences.
Draw a picture of each one.**

clown _____

_____

_____

_____

ringmaster _____

_____

_____

_____

juggler _____

_____

_____

_____

elephant _____

_____

_____

_____

tightrope walker _____

_____

_____

_____

Spell the words. Check yourself.

Spell the words. Check yourself.

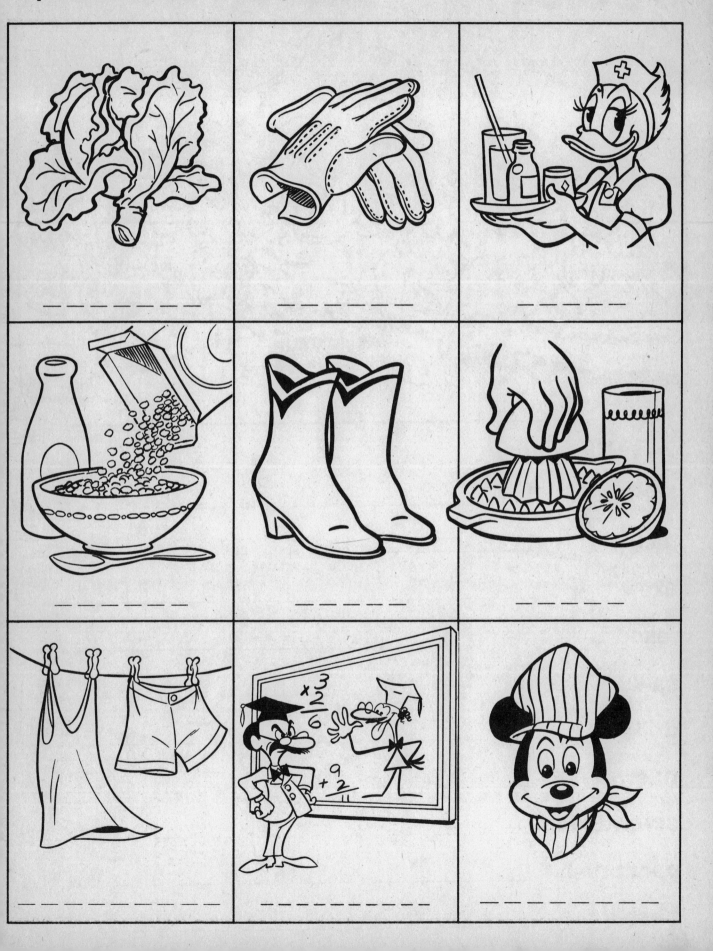

Tools

Write the words.

hammer _____

nail _____

axe _____

rake _____

saw _____

drill _____

ruler _____

screwdriver _____

paintbrush _____

flashlight _____

Spell the words.

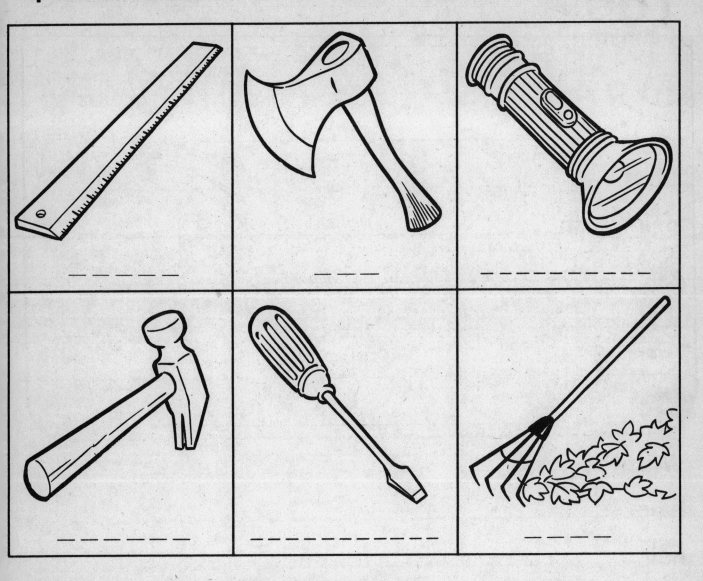

Spell the new words that rhyme with:

| paw | pail | pill |

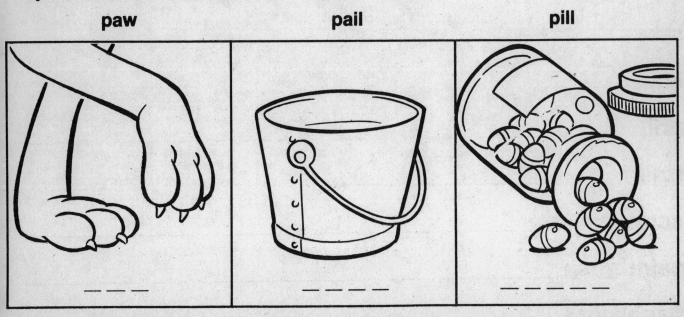

Write a sentence telling what each tool is used for.

flashlight _____

_____

_____

_____

paintbrush _____

_____

_____

_____

axe _____

_____

_____

_____

rake _____

_____

_____

_____

drill _____

_____

_____

Farm

Write the words.

wagon _____

barn _____

field _____

tractor _____

well _____

loft _____

scarecrow _____

horse _____

pig _____

cow _____

Spell the words.

Spell the new words that rhyme with:

bell	wig	plow

Write a sentence for each word.

barn _____

_____

_____

_____

tractor _____

_____

_____

_____

well _____

_____

_____

_____

cow _____

_____

_____

_____

loft _____

_____

_____

_____

Spell the words. Check yourself.

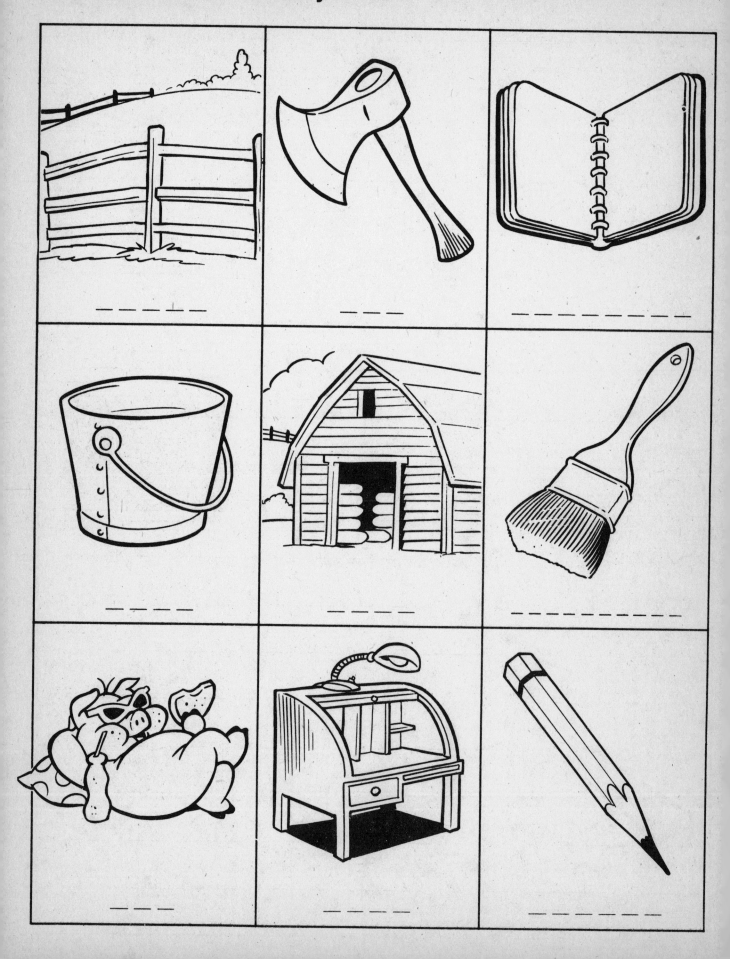

Spell the words. Check yourself.

Birds

Write the words.

nest _____

birdhouse _____

cage _____

beak _____

wing _____

feather _____

fly _____

worm _____

robin _____

crow _____

Spell the words.

— — — — —   — — — — — — —   — — — —

— — — — — — — —   — — — — — — —   — — — —

Spell the new words that rhyme with:

sing   **leak**   **bow**

— — — —   — — — —   — — — —

Write a sentence for each word.

feather _____

_____

_____

_____

fly _____

_____

_____

_____

birdhouse _____

_____

_____

_____

nest _____

_____

_____

_____

worm _____

_____

_____

_____

Sports

Write the words.

football   _____

baseball   _____

basketball   _____

soccer   _____

tennis   _____

hockey   _____

golf   _____

swim   _____

skiing   _____

fishing   _____

Spell the words.

Spell the new words that rhyme with:

trim   dish   jockey

Write a sentence about each sport.

basketball _____

_____

_____

_____

football _____

_____

_____

fish _____

_____

_____

_____

baseball _____

_____

_____

swim _____

_____

_____

Spell the words. Check yourself.

Spell the words. Check yourself.

Weather

Write the words.

rain   _____

sleet   _____

snow   _____

clouds   _____

fog   _____

hail   _____

lightning   _____

weather vane _____

thermometer _____

barometer _____

Spell the words.

Spell the new words that rhyme with:

street　　　　　　　　　**log**　　　　　　　　　**train**

Write about how you feel in the different kinds of weather.

rain _____

_____

_____

_____

snow _____

_____

_____

fog _____

_____

_____

_____

lightning _____

_____

_____

sleet _____

_____

_____

Music

Write the words.

notes _____

instruments _____

conductor _____

orchestra _____

band _____

drum _____

piano _____

violin _____

cymbals _____

horn _____

Spell the words.

Spell the new words that rhyme with:

corn   stand   votes

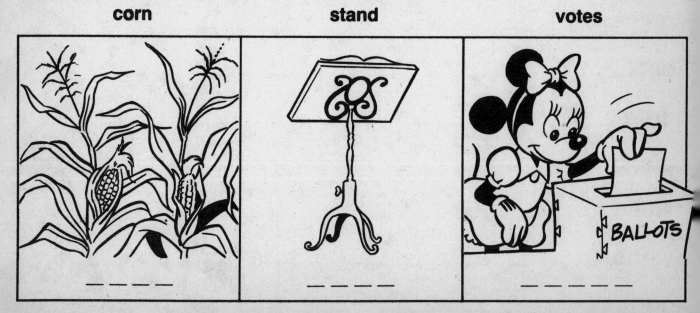